BLUES
HANON

Published by

WISE PUBLICATIONS

14-15 Berners Street, London W1T 3LJ,
United Kingdom.

Exclusive Distributors:

MUSIC SALES LIMITED

Distribution Centre, Newmarket Road, Bury St Edmunds,
Suffolk IP33 3YB, United Kingdom.

MUSIC SALES CORPORATION

257 Park Avenue South, New York, NY 10010, USA.

MUSIC SALES PTY LIMITED

20 Resolution Drive, Caringbah, NSW 2229, Australia.

Order No. AM1004619
ISBN 978-1-78038-522-8
This book © Copyright 2012 Wise Publications,
a division of Music Sales Limited.
This book previously available as AM27889.

Written by Leo Alfassy.
Edited by Brenda Murphy.
Introduction by Graham Vickers.
Cover designed by Michael Bell Design.
Printed in the EU.

BLUESHANON

EXCLUSIVELY DISTRIBUTED BY

London / New York / Paris / Sydney / Copenhagen / Berlin / Madrid / Hong Kong / Tokyo

CONTENTS

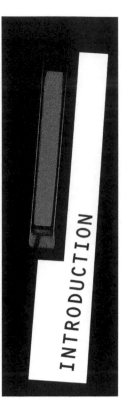

A true American original, the blues was a music form that originated in African-American communities of the Deep South towards the end of the 19th century. It emerged as both a form and a genre, and usually consisted of simple narrative ballads much influenced by spirituals, work songs, and field hollers. Later it would spread geographically as black workers migrated to the North, West and Midwest and this would give rise to various sub-categories of the form. Blues had a profound impact on the development of jazz and boogie-woogie and even influenced certain strands of concert hall music – George Gershwin's 'Rhapsody In Blue' springs to mind, as does Aaron Copland's 'Four Piano Blues.' Eventually it would inform rhythm & blues and, in turn, rock'n'roll too.

Technically speaking the classic blues number is a strophic (verse-repeating) song set to three-line stanzas – that is to say it is easily definable in the language of an existing European music tradition. What sets it apart are several unique African-American characteristics, the main ones being: a melodic line that consists of mostly descending phrases; scales that contain flat sevenths, thirds, and fifths – 'blue' notes; open, expressive vocal styles employing glissandi, melismata and falsettos; and a polyrhythmic interplay between the voice and the accompaniment.

Of the formative elements of the blues, the unstructured field hollers were little more than formalized howls of grievance against harsh conditions; the spirituals injected religious belief, protestation and a blend of African and European melodies; and the work songs imposed a rhythmic element comparable perhaps with the metronomic songs of marching soldiers. If at heart the blues was a political statement, its wider appeal was to be as a series of heartfelt personal expressions of the rootless, exploited and poverty-stricken black population of the American South.

In the early years of the 20th century the agricultural South began to be industrialized and this resulted in the first Great Migration, which resulted in some two million itinerant black workers exchanging one kind of poverty for another as they relocated to the slums of the Northern and Midwestern cities in search of work.

The rural vocal blues, which had rarely had more accompaniment
than basic guitar or harmonica, was transformed into an urban genre
that frequently included a piano among its proliferating instrumentation.
This new urban blues found a home in the juke joints, barrel houses
and rent house parties of the cities where, as dance music, it assumed a
new energy and higher levels of improvisation. Low pay and harsh living
conditions still made the blues the natural medium for black protest,
but now it was also more inclined to embrace sexual topics and dance
crazes while playing to wider and more far-flung audiences.

In 1920, the first blues record by a black vocalist appeared, to be
followed by thousands of 'race' records intended for black radio stations
and black customers. After the war The Second Great Migration saw
African-Americans from the rural south relocating to northern cities where
they represented a growing market for 'race' records (a term which
gradually fell into decline as rhythm & blues emerged as the new
commercial face of the music.) The American South was predictably slower
to respond to change and in the early 1950s the young Elvis Presley was
still listening to 'race' radio stations in order to hear blues records such
as Arthur Crudup's 'That's All Right,' the song that in Presley's cover
version effectively launched white rock'n'roll.

From that point onwards previously unknown or forgotten bluesmen
would become figures of growing interest to musicologists and fans of rock
music alike. Some old bluesmen even survived long enough to enjoy
late-blooming fame. Field hand Mississippi John Hurt (born 1893), who
had rarely played blues for anyone except immediate friends and family,
was rediscovered on the strength of one obscure and unsuccessful record
made in 1928. In the 1960s he was encouraged to record anew and
perform commercially, which he did to great acclaim. The blues, a bleak
rural lament which also spawned boogie-woogie and jazz, was embraced
by successive generations of musicians to become enshrined as one of
the most potent founding elements of modern rock music.

Graham Vickers

The next section explains the characteristic features of the blues in relation to the basic elements of music. This is followed by thirty-three practical exercises, each dealing with a specific technical problem for the left or right hand. In order to acquire an absolute independence of hands, it is necessary to practice each hand separately. This should be done in a slow tempo and without the use of the right pedal. Instead, the student can keep a steady tempo by tapping the beat with his right foot.

Elements of Blues Style

Melody

The blues began as a lamentory chant with irregular phrase structure and free rhythm. Gradually, it developed into a simple repetitious twelve-bar melody, consisting of three brooding descending phrases with a driving rhythmic accompaniment. Each musical phrase corresponds to one line of the three-line blues stanza, with an instrumental interlude.

Often one or more initial eighth notes precede the phrases in the form of an upbeat.

In order to follow the changing harmony, the musical phrases can be altered chromatically (a), or transposed to another pitch above or below (b).

The melodic line of the blues cannot be judged in the same way as that of a classical piece, or even in the same way as another kind of popular melody. It furnishes only the framework for creative improvisations and ceaseless embellishments; the performer being more or less the spontaneous composer.

Harmony and Form

The harmonic and formal structures of the blues and the boogie are the same. Every composition consists of a succession of twelve-bar sections called "choruses," each section containing an identical harmonic pattern. This pattern is based on the triads built over the first (tonic), fourth (subdominant), and fifth (dominant) degrees of the scale. Here is the formal and harmonic structure of a typical blues or boogie in the key of C.

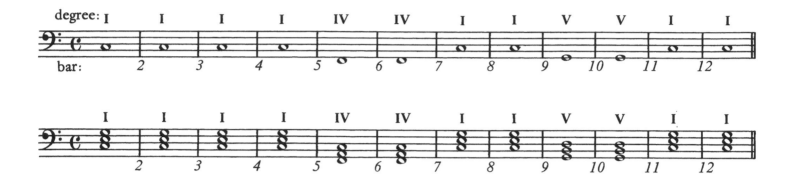

Sometimes the tonic triads of measures 2 and 10 are replaced by the subdominant triad or a minor seventh chord.

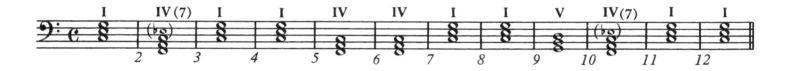

There are many exceptions to this basic harmonic pattern. The great performers of blues and boogie use sophisticated chords, tone clusters, and strikingly original progressions within this fundamental framework. Here is a modern version of the blues (or boogie) form.

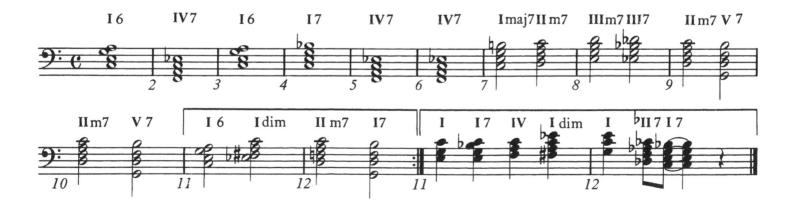

Bass Line

The development of a good left-hand technique is essential in blues playing because of the twofold importance of the bass line: as a harmonic support, and as a replacement for the rhythm section of a band. A simple bass figure can consist of the repetition of open fifths or chords.

The bass line can also consist of the so-called "walking bass" (notes "walking" up and down a scale or in broken chords), probably derived from the common bass patterns of jazz bassists.

Here are some other typical bass figures.

Blue Notes and Scales

The melodic line often contains features typical of the blues, namely the so-called "blue" notes. These are notes, particularly the third, fifth, and seventh degrees of the scale, whose intonation lies *between* the major and minor pitches. (For practical purposes, these degrees are flatted by a semitone.) In blues singing, these notes could be easily "bent" or "glided" by the singer or played on the guitar, the most important instrument for blues accompaniment. In order to imitate the blue notes, which were impossible to play on a keyboard instrument, the blues pianists had to develop a special technique of embellishments consisting of grace notes and slides.

Although most blues melodies are based on the major scale, some use other scales such as tonal or semitonal pentatonic scales, or "blues scales" containing the blue notes. Tonal pentatonic scales consist of only five notes and include no semitones.

The last inversion of the above example is quite often used in blues, especially in a descending line.

Semitonal pentatonic scales include semitones.

The blues scale adds blue notes to the major scale but omits the second, sixth, and major seventh degrees.

Sometimes blues pianists use a minor triad in the right hand and a major triad in the left hand simultaneously.

Meter and Tempo

The meter of the blues, like most jazz music, is **C** (common). Often the second and fourth beats of the bar (backbeats) are heavily accentuated. Some pieces are in $\frac{6}{8}$ or $\frac{12}{8}$ meters, partly under the influence of gospel songs.

The blues and the boogie-woogie have much in common: the formal structure, the chordal sequence, and some bass figures. But there are certain differences, two of them being the tempo and the dynamics. Since the blues is originally a song of lamentation describing a life close to the bone, it is usually in a slow tempo and on a medium dynamic level. On the other hand, the boogie is a heavily percussive piano style with great rhythmic vitality. It is played in a fast tempo on a quite high dynamic level.

Exercises

1.

2.

3.

4.

Syncopation

The next exercise introduces a very important device in jazz, syncopation. Syncopation is, generally speaking, any deliberate displacement of the natural accent from a strong to a weak beat. In western music, every bar contains strong and weak beats. In $\frac{4}{4}$ meter, the first and third beats are strong; in $\frac{3}{4}$ meter, only the first. Example (a) shows the natural accents in $\frac{4}{4}$ and $\frac{3}{4}$ meters. Example (b) illustrates the displacement of these accents.

Jazz especially uses syncopations on shorter time values (eighth and sixteenth notes), which creates a complete imbalance in the listener's feeling of rhythmic security and excitement.

In classical music, the proper way to perform a syncopation is to accentuate it heavily. The jazzman softens these accents by prolonging the value of the shorter note and playing it almost as long as the syncopated note. For instance:

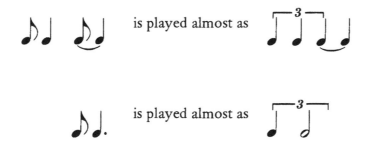

17

5.

Parallel Thirds and Sixths (Right Hand)

Exercises 6 through 9 deal with thirds; exercises 11 through 13 deal with sixths in the right hand. Parallel thirds and sixths are difficult to perform evenly; the two component keys must be struck precisely together. I recommend the major and minor scales as preparatory introduction to these exercises.

6.

7.

8.

9.

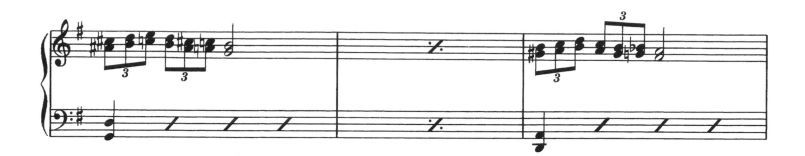

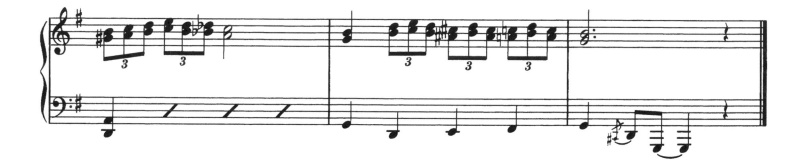

Blue Notes

The next exercise introduces blue notes. As explained previously, the blue notes occur mostly on the third, fifth, and seventh degrees of the scale, which are flatted. Often one hand plays a major triad while the other one plays a minor chord. This is, of course, done purposely.

10.

11.

12.

27

13.

Grace Notes

In classical music, the time value of a grace note (note printed in small type) must be subtracted from that of the preceding or following notes. In the interpretation of blues, the value of the grace note is extremely short—in other words, the grace note and the adjacent note are played almost simultaneously *on* the beat. This extremely short value is achieved through the sliding of the same finger from a black to a white key on the keyboard.

Because it is impossible to slide with the same finger from one white to another white key, or from a white to a black key, two fingers are necessary to perform the grace note and the adjacent note.

To create an even greater illusion of guitar playing, the blues pianist often strikes simultaneously two notes situated a semitone apart (a). The agglomeration of a few semitones in the same chord, called "tone cluster," adds more excitement to the music (b).

14.

15.

As mentioned before, a jazz musician softens syncopated and dotted notes. In the next exercise, the dotted eighth-sixteenth-note figure ♫ should be played as ♪. In this way, the ♫ rhythm in the right hand will fall together with the ♫ figure in the left hand.

16.

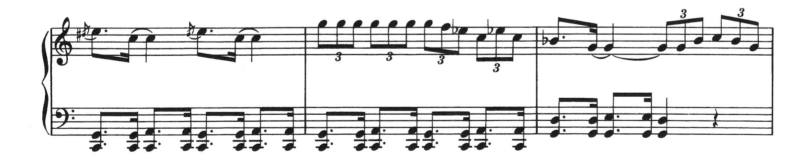

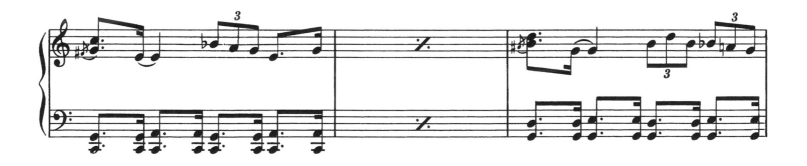

Tremolo

The tremolo is a device frequently used in blues. It occurs in the form of quickly repeated notes, mostly thirds and octaves.

Sometimes the tremolo consists of whole chords, performed with one or both hands (a). Very often it is preceded by grace notes or slurs (b).

17.

18.

Parallel Sixths (Left Hand)

The next exercise deals with sixths in the left hand. As in the previous exercises for
the right hand, one should pay special attention to the smooth transition from one sixth
to another and to the sounding of the two keys at precisely the same moment.

19.

20.

Left-Hand Extension—Tenths

Physical limitations restrict the stretch of many hands. The present study will be helpful in the gradual extension of the grasp of the left hand, but it should not be practiced excessively.

21.

22.

Compound Meter

Many blues are written in compound meter: $\frac{6}{8}$ or $\frac{12}{8}$. The subdivision of the eighth note into sixteenths and thirty-seconds creates problems in sight reading. The next exercise is a very helpful introduction to these meters. It contains two parts, A and B, which are identical with the exception that the first part is written in common meter, and the second in compound meter. The student is advised to compare the note values of the first section with those of the second, which should *sound* the same.

23. A

24.

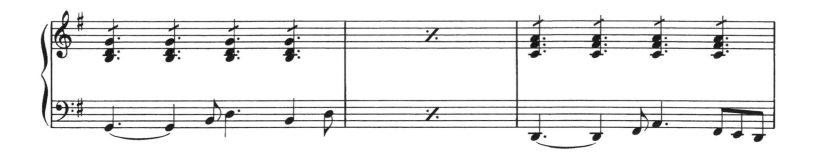

25.

(bass solo)

26.

27.

28.

29.

30.

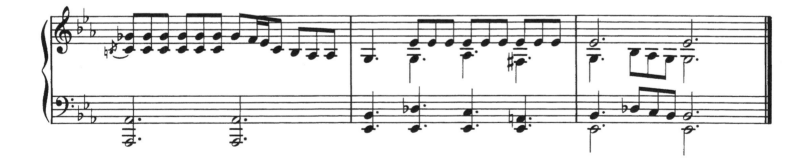

31.

32.

33.

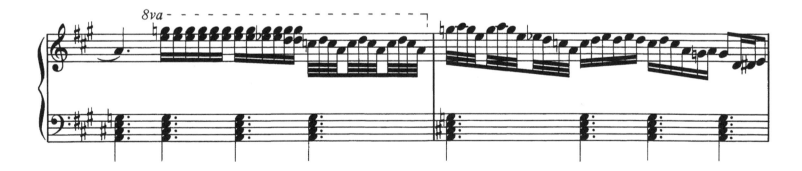